God's Great Plan
STORYBOOK BIBLE

{ For God loved the world so much that he gave his
only Son. God gave his Son so that whoever believes
in him may not be lost, but have eternal life. }

John 3:16 ICB

Tommy NELSON®

An Imprint of Thomas Nelson
thomasnelson.com

In the beginning, there was nothing to see,
No sun or mountain, no bird or tree.
God spoke the words and all was bright.
God called it day, and He called the darkness night.

Genesis 1:1–5

God saw it was good, and He had good plans.
Nothing was made out of pure chance.

God made the sun, the stars, and the moon.
Some shone at night and others at noon.
Flowers bloomed and birds sang their songs.
Monkeys climbed trees and ants moved along.

Genesis 1:14-25

God made it all; it was a choice.
All of creation obeyed His voice.

The world was perfect, but needed one thing:
Someone to jump and dance and sing.
God made one man and one woman with His loving care,
And He gave Adam and Eve a garden to share.

Genesis 1:26-31

In the garden God walked with His children a while,
With laughter and joy and happy smiles.

There were plenty of trees from which they could eat.
There were small sour berries and cherries so sweet.
There was fruit from one tree, and God said, "Don't even try.
If you eat from it, you will most certainly die."

The snake did not care about God's commands.
He had something evil and wicked planned.
Eve was tricked by the snake and ate fruit from the tree.
Adam ate too, and the snake watched them with glee.

Genesis 3:1–7

God's heart was broken as he sent Adam and Eve off His land.
But in His mind He had a salvation plan.

As we have learned, it didn't take long
For Adam and Eve to do what was wrong.
Years passed by and the world was a mess.
People said "No!" to God, and to evil they said "Yes!"

This made God angry and so very sad,
But there was one man who made His heart glad.
God said, "Noah, build an ark! Listen to me!
From a great flood I will save you and your family."

Genesis 6:5-22

Noah trusted in God and started to labor,
Even though he was teased and mocked by his neighbor.

Once safe in the ark, God closed the door.
Forty days and nights, it rained and it poured.
Noah wondered, When will the flood be over?
Then he saw that the waters had started to lower.

At long last on dry land, their hearts filled with joy.
God had been with the animals, the girls, and the boys.
The animals marched out in a long, happy row.
Then they praised God for His promise and His rainbow.

Genesis 7–8

God's promise to Noah was hard to miss.
He said, "Never again will I flood the earth like this!"

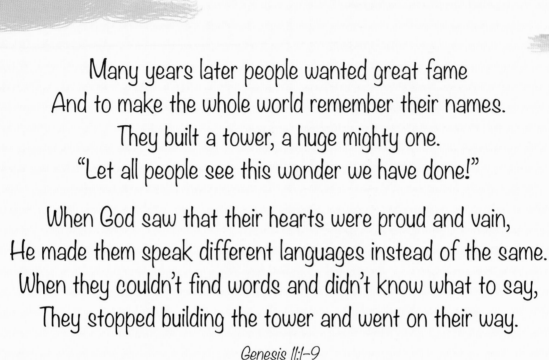

Many years later people wanted great fame
And to make the whole world remember their names.
They built a tower, a huge mighty one.
"Let all people see this wonder we have done!"

When God saw that their hearts were proud and vain,
He made them speak different languages instead of the same.
When they couldn't find words and didn't know what to say,
They stopped building the tower and went on their way.

Genesis 11:1-9

God wanted to be the one they adored,
But they didn't want to make Him their Lord.

God still loved the world, and He still had a plan.
He wanted a people, so He first chose a man.
God said, "Abraham, you'll be the father of many!"
Abraham asked, "How God? Because children . . . I do not have any?"

Genesis 12:2 & 15:1–6

But God meant every word that He said.
Throughout the whole world, His children would spread.

God said, "Go to a place I will show you one day."
Abraham obeyed and was soon on his way.
With Sarah, his wife, and all that they owned,
With their household and animals, the left their home.

Genesis 12:1–9

Abraham trusted that God had taken his hand.
And sooner or later He would lead them to His land.

"Look at the stars," God said one night.
"Can you count them? Please try, and use all your might.
You'll have children, more than the stars you can see."
Abraham had faith that all God said would be.

Genesis 15:1–6; 21:1–7

And so God kept the promise He gave to His friend.
Abraham and Sarah had baby Isaac, and their family began.

Isaac married years later and had twin boys.
Esau was wild, and Jacob home with his toys.
Jacob was quiet, but he thought he knew best.
With animal fur on his arms and on his chest,
Jacob went to his father and said, "I am Esau, dear Dad.
I brought you the food that makes you so glad.
Now, give me your blessing and all that is mine!"
Isaac was blind, so he thought it was fine.

Genesis 25:21-34; 27:1-46

Isaac then gave to Jacob what was Esau's treasure.
He gave him great blessings beyond any measure.

Now Esau got angry, and Jacob ran for his life.
In a country far off, he chose Rachel for his wife.
Rachel's father was sneaky and a bit tricky and wild.
He married off Jacob to his other child.

Jacob still wanted Rachel and married her later.
His family then grew from small to greater.
Twelve sons and a daughter for whom he took care.
There was always enough for the family to share.

Genesis 27:41-28:3; 29; 30:22-24

God blessed Jacob with a beautiful family.
They tried to be all that God wanted them to be.

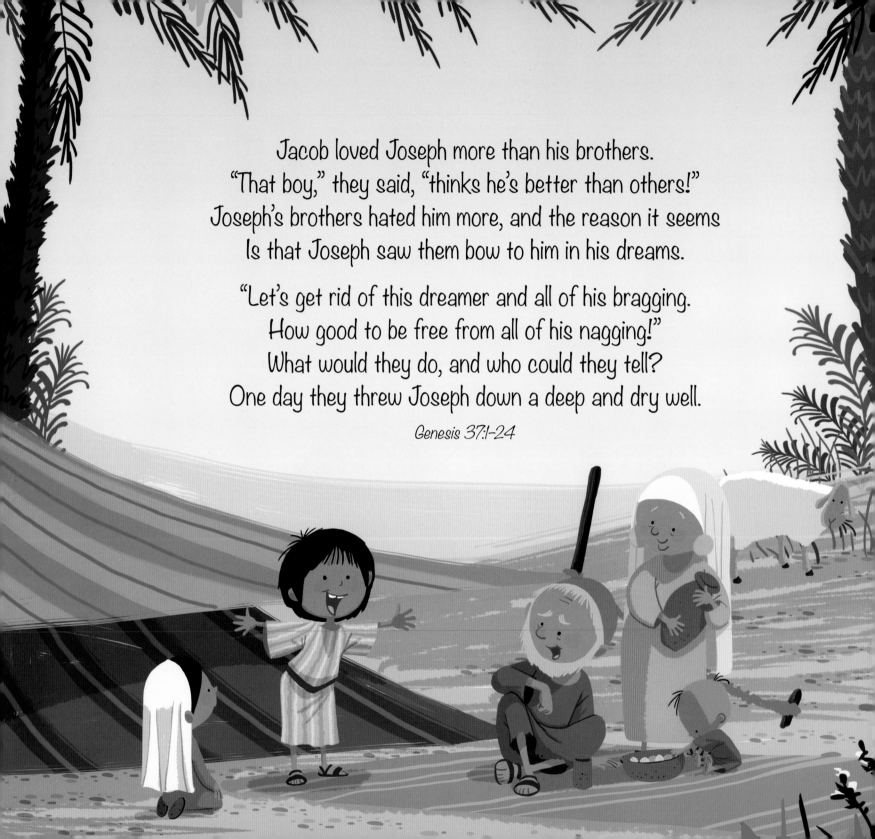

Jacob loved Joseph more than his brothers.
"That boy," they said, "thinks he's better than others!"
Joseph's brothers hated him more, and the reason it seems
Is that Joseph saw them bow to him in his dreams.

"Let's get rid of this dreamer and all of his bragging.
How good to be free from all of his nagging!"
What would they do, and who could they tell?
One day they threw Joseph down a deep and dry well.

Genesis 37:1-24

"He was killed by a beast!" They told their father lies.
But God heard it all, and it was no surprise.

The well could have been Joseph's grave,
But the brothers instead sold him off as a slave.
Joseph traveled alone for miles in the sand,
But God held him safely with His mighty hand.

In Egypt they sold him again as a slave,
But Joseph was good; in fact he was brave.
All that he did, he did with such skill
That everyone loved him and showed him good will.

Genesis 37:25–36; 39:1–5

God was with Joseph and gave him great favor.
God knew that Joseph would be a lifesaver.

One day they said that Joseph had failed.
Though he was blameless, he wound up in jail.
But even in jail he made some new friends.
With wisdom and faith, he knew this was not the end.

"Listen to this dream," said two prisoners one morning.
Joseph said to them, "Your dreams are a warning.
One would be free, and the other man not."
His words came true; he understood a lot.

Genesis 39:19–40:23

"I'll help you out," said the man who was freed.
But soon he'd forgotten what he and Joseph had agreed.

Then Pharaoh had a dream, and he was afraid.
"Bring in the wise men," he said, "and don't wait!"
But none of the wise men understood the dream.
"Bring Joseph," said someone, "his wisdom is keen."

And so they brought Joseph to help mighty Pharaoh.
Joseph reported what God let him know.
"Oh, king, this is what your dream is about:
Seven years of plenty, then seven of drought."

Genesis 41

The king now made Joseph the top man in charge.
This was God's doing by far and by large.

Jacob sent his sons to Egypt for grain.
They had no food because there was no rain.
They did not recognize their own little brother.
In fact, they thought he was another.

Joseph was harsh, and he said they were spies.
"You say you are brothers, but is this all lies?"
Joseph knew who they were, and he wanted to know
If they felt bad for their actions from a long time ago.

Genesis 42:1-22

"We are being punished," they said in a low voice.
"We shouldn't have hurt Joseph. We had a choice."

Then later one day Joseph told them at last,
"I am your brother, whom you sold in the past.
You sold me off to a traveling merchant's caravan.
But all the while it was part of God's mighty plan."

"You meant to harm me, but God meant it for good.
Bring back my father, now. I ask that you would
Please stay here in Egypt and make it your own.
I'm grateful to God for the mercy He's shown."

Genesis 45

Their hearts were all softened and mended,
And the hate for their brother now ended.

After many years and Joseph was gone,
The people forgot all that Joseph had done.
Along came a Pharaoh who sat on the throne
And made the Israelites slaves that he owned.

One mother decided to save her small boy.
He was precious to her and brought her such joy.
She made a basket, and it floated a while.
A princess found the baby there on the Nile.

Exodus 1:1–2:10

She named him Moses and had no idea
God would use him greatly, in spite of his fear.

Moses grew up in the palace, but his people were slaves.
One day he saw a slave and an Egyptian misbehave.
Moses got angry, and he put an end to the fight.
He did not speak calmly but instead used his might.

Moses killed the Egyptian man.
Then he feared for his life, so he ran and he ran.
He wound up a shepherd, though he was a prince.
And the murder he regretted ever since.

Exodus 2:10–25

Moses had children, and he had a wife.
Maybe he wondered, "Is this now my life?"

Then one day a bush was aflame.
Moses thought, The sun is to blame!
But it wasn't the sun who had called his name out.
From the bush Moses heard God speak aloud.

"My people," said God, "are suffering in pain!
I want you to lead them from Egypt again."
"But who am I to bring forth this request?"
Moses asked although God's patience he'd test.

"Throw on the ground the staff in your hand,
And then pick it up again if you can!"
Moses did so and his staff turned into a snake.
Only God the Almighty such a wonder could make.

Exodus 3-4

Moses traveled through miles of sand.
Just as Joseph had traveled toward Egypt's land.

But Pharaoh said "No! No slave will be free!
There's no way on earth that I will agree!"
However, there was and God knew just how
He could make the wicked Egyptian king bow.

God sent ten plagues, and His might He showed.
Then at last Pharaoh said to the slaves, "You can go!"
The king was strong, but the true King is stronger.
Pharaoh, at last, could resist God no longer.

Exodus 7:14–12:38

The Israelites then packed and left in a hurry.
God won them their freedom. Why now would they worry?

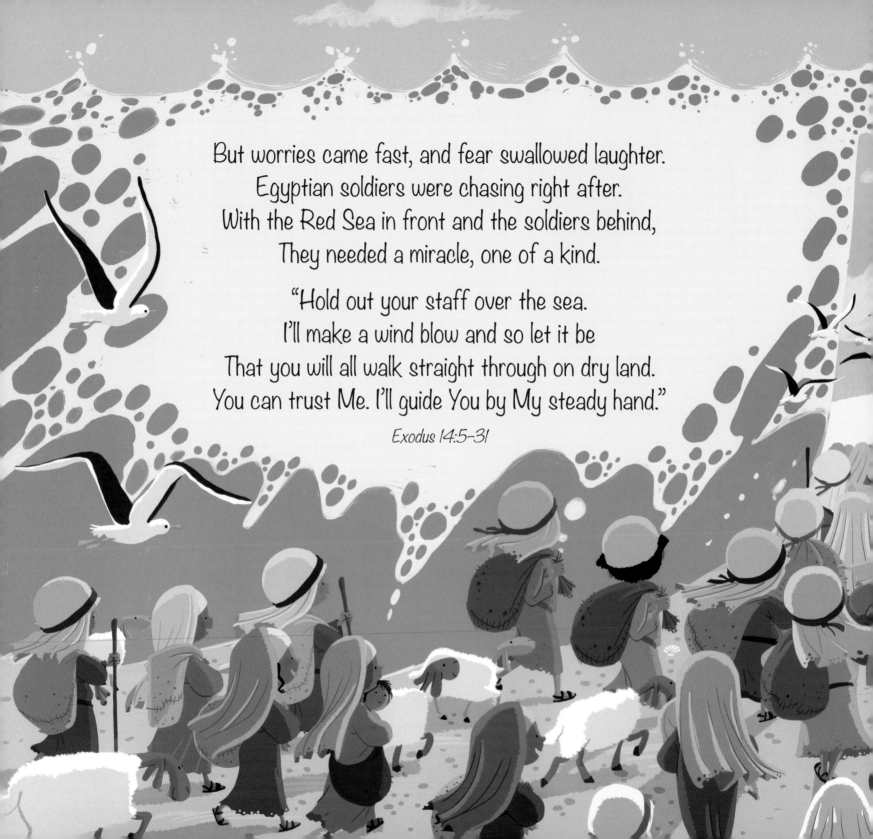

But worries came fast, and fear swallowed laughter.
Egyptian soldiers were chasing right after.
With the Red Sea in front and the soldiers behind,
They needed a miracle, one of a kind.

"Hold out your staff over the sea.
I'll make a wind blow and so let it be
That you will all walk straight through on dry land.
You can trust Me. I'll guide You by My steady hand."

Exodus 14:5-31

So God let a wind part the waters at night.
Not a thing is too hard for His glorious might.

When food was scarce, the people complained,
"Oh, leaving Egypt has all been in vain!"
"Stop grumbling!" said Moses. "Today you'll have meat.
By morning you'll have all the bread you can eat."

At night, God sent birds for the people to catch.
And then in the morning, He sent batch by batch
The sweetest of dew—the soft manna flakes.
It was so delicious, like newly baked cakes.

Exodus 16

Day by day they saw God's good deeds.
He graciously provided for everyone's needs.

Moses went up on Mount Sinai alone.
He went to meet God, who would cut out in stone
The Ten Commandments, and this was God's law.
When God spoke to Moses, he was truly in awe.

There were ten rules, but they said this in short:
Love God with your whole heart, for He is your Lord.
Love your neighbor, your friend, and the stranger you meet,
And care for all others as for your own needs.

Exodus 19:16–20:21; 34:29–35

Moses went down with the tablets of stone.
His face was bright, and it brilliantly shone.

But Oh! What was this? What had they done?
A mighty big feast the people had begun.
They danced all around a calf made of gold.
"They praised it as god!" Moses was told.

Moses was angry. "Stop this terrible sin!"
God loved them, but they turned their backs on Him.
Moses shattered the calf and told them just why,
"To believe it's a god is a sin and a lie!"

Exodus 32

The people regretted and said, "We'll obey!
From now on we'll listen and stay on the way!"

In a beautiful chest lay the law and commands.
They carried it carefully through hot desert sands.
And God led them faithfully by His great hand,
Not quickly, but surely to the Promised Land.

Deuteronomy 34

And when Moses died, it made them all grieve,
But first God chose Joshua to be the lead.

When at long last they came to the land they would take,
They met strong walls of stone, which no one could break.
"Walk around the city," said God, "and make no sound!
But on the seventh day, SHOUT! Watch the walls fall to the ground!"

Joshua 6

Jericho was the first fight of many.
The foes did not win, not one, not any.

The people soon wanted a king of their own.
They'd forgotten that God was the One on the throne.
God said to Samuel, "Then give them this king!
They will soon discover their choice has a sting."

Samuel then told them what a king would demand,
"Your sons will be his soldiers, and he'll want the fruits of your land."
"This doesn't matter!" said the people with ease.
They forgot who it was that they really should please.

1 Samuel 8; 10:20–26; 13:1–12

Samuel chose Saul; he looked very strong.
But his heart was too weak, so he did what was wrong.

The Philistine army got ready for war.
Goliath the giant was shouting and swore,
"Send one man to fight me, but I'm sure he will lose."
But no Israelite soldier had courage to use.

Then a shepherd boy, David, came passing by.
He felt very angry. "Who is this guy?
I'll do battle with him, like I fought with a bear.
I fear not his words. I don't easily scare."

1 Samuel 17:1–50

David slew the giant, who fell like a tower.
David won with God's help and backed by His power.

As the years came and went, the people changed like waves.
Sometimes they followed idols, and sometimes the God who saves.
God sent His prophets to teach and remind,
"Please turn back to God. Don't be foolish and blind!"

So the people would turn from their evil behavior
And trust in God as their one, true Savior.
Sometimes this continued for years or a decade,
But their love for God would again later fade.

Judges 2:16-19

God said, "Choose Me. Please don't be feeble.
You know I chose you to be My special people!"

The people kept falling away from God's word.
They seemed to have trouble remembering what they'd heard.
God had warned if they scorned His advice,
It wouldn't be easy, and it would come with a price.

The price was this: they'd be forced to leave.
Then surely their sin they greatly would grieve.
God's people were forced into a strange land.
Soon they would bow at another king's command.

2 Kings 23:31-37; 25:1-21

God had not forgotten, and He still had a plan.
He'd save them and bring them all back to their land.

Four hundred years later, after a very long time,
God sent an angel to a girl in her prime.
"Greetings, dear Mary!" said the angel with joy.
"You're loved by our God and will soon have a boy!"

"But, I am not married. I don't have a man!"
"God will do this because it is His great plan.
His name will be Jesus, and He's God's only Son."
"I believe you," said Mary, "His will must be done!"

Luke 1:26-38; Matthew 1:18-25

Mary and Joseph were soon to be married.
So she went and told him about the baby she carried.

Later they traveled to Bethlehem town,
But they had no place to lay their heads down.
Then finding a stable, "Go there!" said a stranger.
It was here that God's Son was born in a manger.

Shepherds had heard from angels, very large hosts.
At first they were scared; they thought they were ghosts.
"Peace," said the angels, and they started to sing.
"You'll find in a manger, your Savior, your King!"

Luke 2:1–20

The night was dark, but a star in the sky
Was shining so brightly, some might have wondered why.

When Jesus was twelve, there was a big feast.
They would have a grand time, for some days at least.
After the feast, they all traveled back.
His family lost sight of Jesus and thought He'd follow their track.

In the temple sat Jesus, asking tough questions.
The teachers were amazed at all His suggestions!
His parents soon found Him with men they called wise.
They asked, "Why did You stay here? That wasn't so nice!"

Luke 2:41-52

Jesus replied, "This is where I should stay!"
But He did as they asked and did not disobey.

Many years later, before His work had begun,
Jesus went to the Jordan to see His cousin John.
There He was baptized, and as soon as He rose,
A voice spoke from heaven, and they heard it so close.

Matthew 3:13–17

"This is My Son, the One whom I love!"
The Spirit of God flew down as a dove.

Two brothers were fishing and saw Jesus one day.
He said, "Follow Me. I'll show you the way!"
The men, Peter and Andrew, dropped their nets and were gone.
Then they added two more named James and John.

Matthew 4:18–22

"Follow Me!" Jesus said, and the twelve men said yes.
Later they saw how many their good work would bless.

In Cana a wedding lasted for hours,
And here Jesus showed for the first time His powers.
"There's no more wine, and it's a disaster!"
"What can be done?" asked the banquet master.

Jesus who worked with God in creation
Asked for water in jars, and with no hesitation
The jars were filled, and the taste was "so fine!"
For Jesus had turned the water to wine.

John 2:1–11

The disciples knew Jesus was the Divine.
The true Son of God had come in their time!

At a well in Samaria a woman came with her jar.
She had walked from the village, and it was not very far.
There Jesus greeted her out of the blue,
"May I have some water? I'm thirsty too."

She was surprised to put it mildly.
Jews and Samaritans disliked each other wildly.
But Jesus didn't care what people said.
"I am the Messiah, so you don't need to fret."

"I'll give you water like a well in your heart."
"That's great!" said the woman. "That is very smart."
"This water," said Jesus, "is not what we drink.
It's great joy forever, far better than you think."

John 4:1–26

The woman ran to the town, and she ran very bold.
"I've met the Messiah, of whom we were told!"

A man who was sick and could not walk
Was carried to Jesus, who was giving a talk.
Failing to squeeze the sick man through the door,
His friends made a plan, which would take a bit more.

They would carefully lower their friend through the roof,
And to Jesus this act of faith was the proof.
"My friend, you are forgiven," He said to the lame.
From that moment on, he was never the same.

Matthew 9:1–8

"Pick up your mat and walk on your feet."
The man, by His word, could now walk down the street.

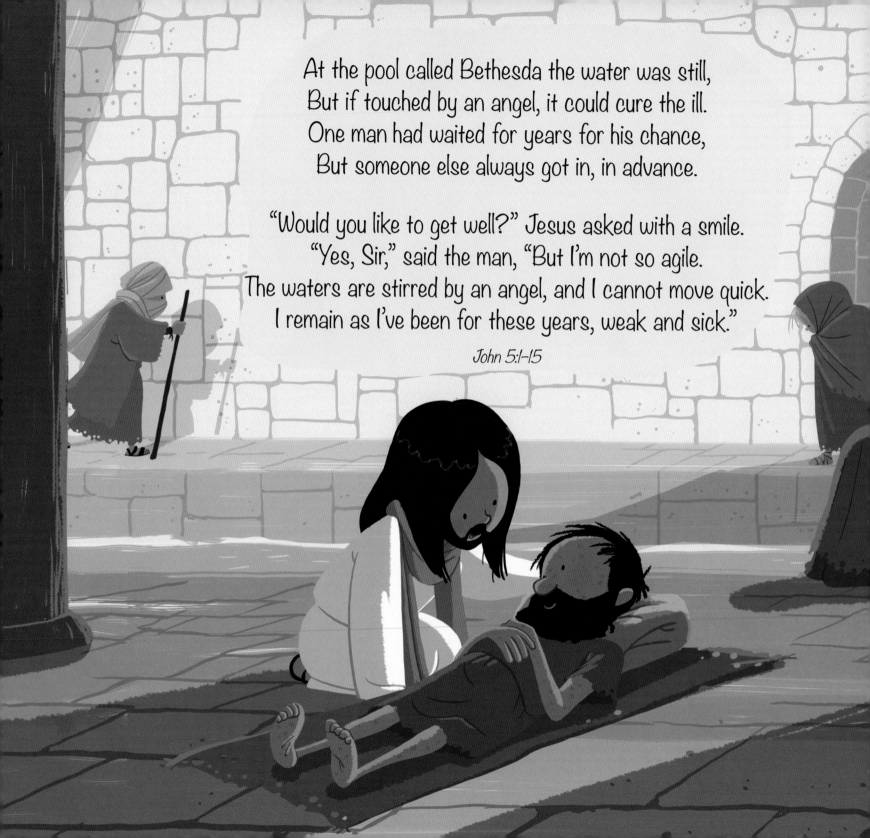

At the pool called Bethesda the water was still,
But if touched by an angel, it could cure the ill.
One man had waited for years for his chance,
But someone else always got in, in advance.

"Would you like to get well?" Jesus asked with a smile.
"Yes, Sir," said the man, "But I'm not so agile.
The waters are stirred by an angel, and I cannot move quick.
I remain as I've been for these years, weak and sick."

John 5:1–15

"Get up and walk," said Jesus, quite straight.
And that's what he did; the man went home through the gate.

Next this happened, ten men came and pleaded,
"Oh, Jesus, Master, heal us. We need it!"
Jesus said, "Go, show yourself to all the priests."
They went on their way, and they had faith at least.

On the way to the priests they were healed, all ten!
But just one, a Samaritan, came to Jesus again.
"Thank You, Lord Jesus. I'm well. I'm made new!"
"Were not all healed?" He asked. "Or was it just you?"

Luke 17:11–19

"Rise and go! Your faith made you well!"
Where the other nine went, no one could tell.

Jesus was teaching a crowd far from town.
They were still there as the sun went down.
"Send them away," said His friends. "They need food."
Jesus said, "You feed them because this is what you should do!"

"But we can't buy food for 5,000 plus."
Then a boy shared his lunch, without any fuss.
Jesus thanked God and broke the bread, piece by piece.
Their hunger soon vanished, and their hunger did cease.

John 6:1–15

This was a miracle; it was plain to see.
"He must be the Prophet!" they all could agree.

Jesus taught about a man who traveled through dangers.
He was attacked and beaten by strangers.
Two priestly men were too busy to care.
"This man is unclean, so why would we dare?"

A Samaritan traveler, though despised by some,
To the beaten man's aid he would soon come.
He cleansed his wounds and brought him along.
He cared for his new friend until he was strong.

Luke 10:30-37

"This is true love!" Jesus said to the crowd.
"Go, do the same. This makes God so proud!"

People brought kids to Jesus to touch.
The disciples, however, thought, "This is too much!"
They started to push the children away.
"Don't bother the Master. Now be on your way!"
When Jesus saw this, it made Him quite mad.
"Don't stop the children. This makes My heart sad!

Mark 10:13-16

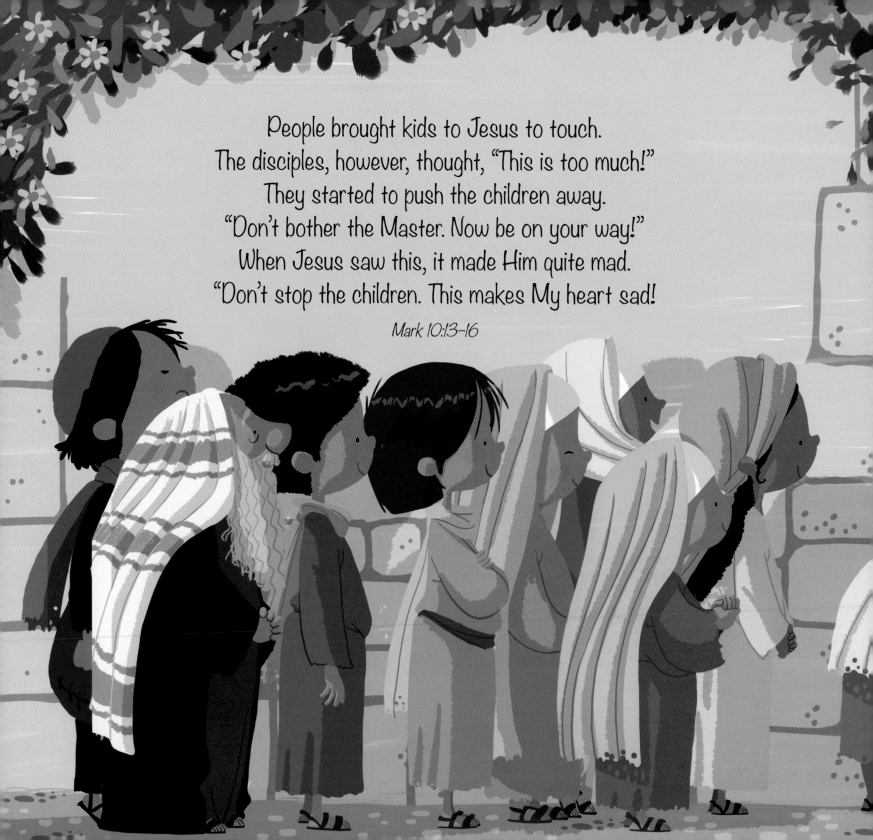

"Children belong to My Kingdom, that's right!"
Jesus then blessed them with all of His might.

"Look at the flowers, so beautifully dressed.
Don't go around worried and hopelessly stressed!
If God dresses the flowers, which dry up in air,
He will give you the clothing that you need to wear."

"Look at the bird. It sows not, neither reaps.
Yet God in His hands, the bird safely He keeps.
Seek first God's kingdom and His will for your life,
And your time on this earth will be filled with less strife."

Matthew 6:25-34

"God in heaven hears when you pray.
Wherever you are, wherever you stay."

To Jerusalem came Jesus on a young donkey's back.
The coats of the people were laid in His track.
They shouted with joy, "Hail, David's Son!"
They did not understand what had just begun.

Matthew 21:1–11

He was a king, but not like they supposed.
He wanted their hearts, but they were all closed.

Jesus would have a last meal with His friends.
This brought them great sadness, but later joys would begin.
Jesus broke into pieces, some bread that He had.
"My body will break, too, but one day your hearts will be glad."

"One of you will betray Me, and it will come with great price."
"You cannot mean me," said Judas, with guilt in his eyes.
He had stolen from others, and it was not just to borrow.
"Yes, it's you!" Jesus said, as His heart filled with sorrow.

Matthew 26:14-30

To tell on Jesus, Judas went during the meal.
For thirty pieces of silver, he had made a rash deal.

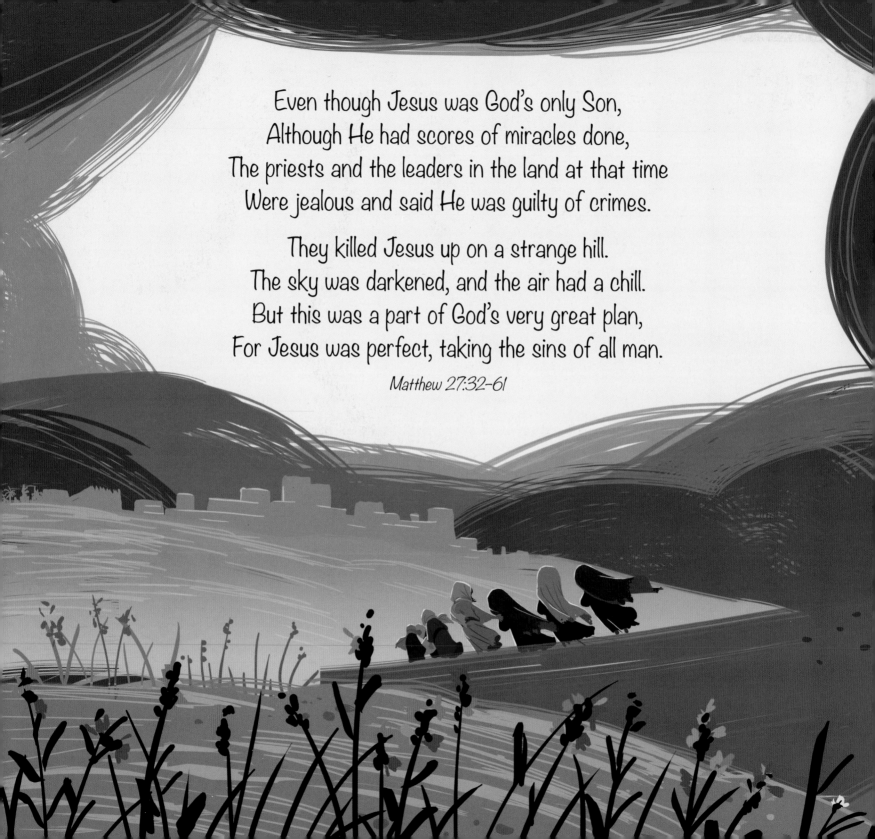

Even though Jesus was God's only Son,
Although He had scores of miracles done,
The priests and the leaders in the land at that time
Were jealous and said He was guilty of crimes.

They killed Jesus up on a strange hill.
The sky was darkened, and the air had a chill.
But this was a part of God's very great plan,
For Jesus was perfect, taking the sins of all man.

Matthew 27:32–61